Harbor
Donald Crews

 Greenwillow Books, New York

Printed in the United
States of America
First Edition
10 9 8 7 6 5 4 3 2 1

Library of Congress
Cataloging in
Publication Data

Crews, Donald. Harbor.
Summary: Presents
various kinds of
boats which come and
go in a busy harbor.
1. Ships—Pictorial
works—Juvenile
literature.
[1. Harbors. 2. Boats] I. Title.
VM307.C8   623.8′2′00222   81-6607
ISBN 0-688-00861-5   AACR2
ISBN 0-688-00862-3 (lib. bdg.)

To the women in my life
& Malcolm

A harbor.

Wharves, docks, piers, and warehouses.

A port for ships,
boats, and cargo.

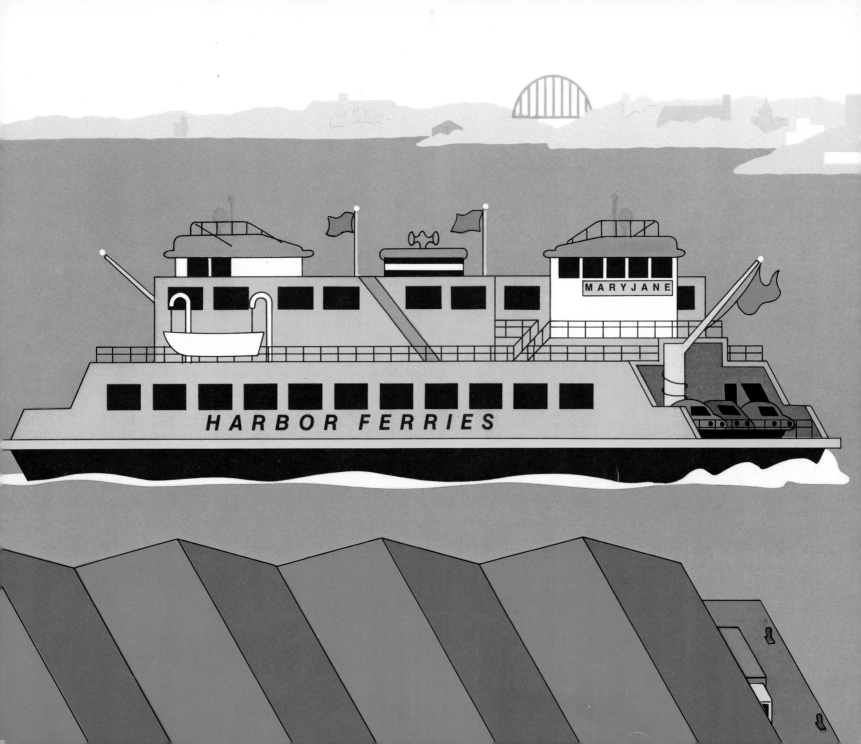

Ferryboats shuttle back and forth from shore to shore.
They do not need to turn around.
The back becomes the front.

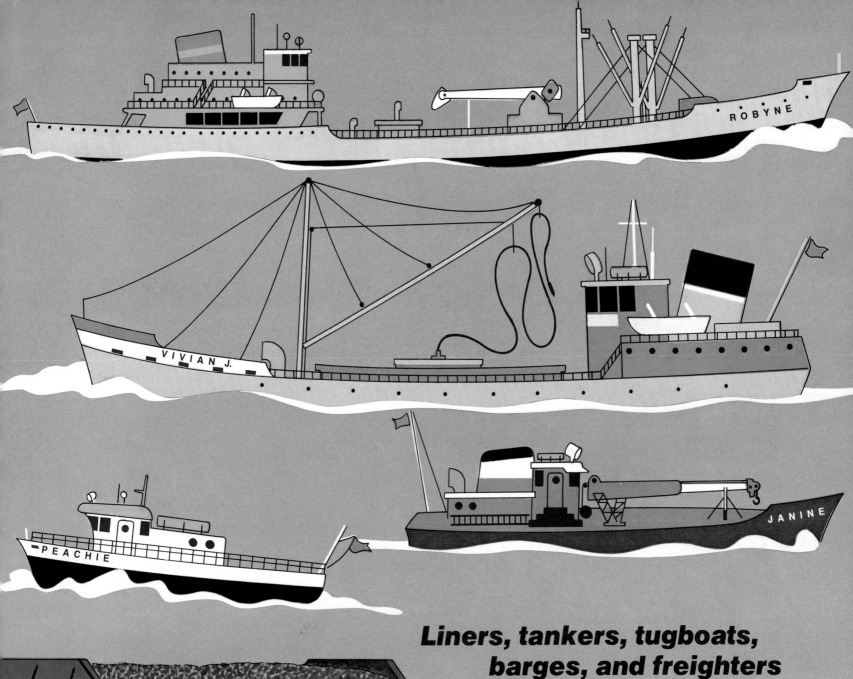

Liners, tankers, tugboats, barges, and freighters move in and out.

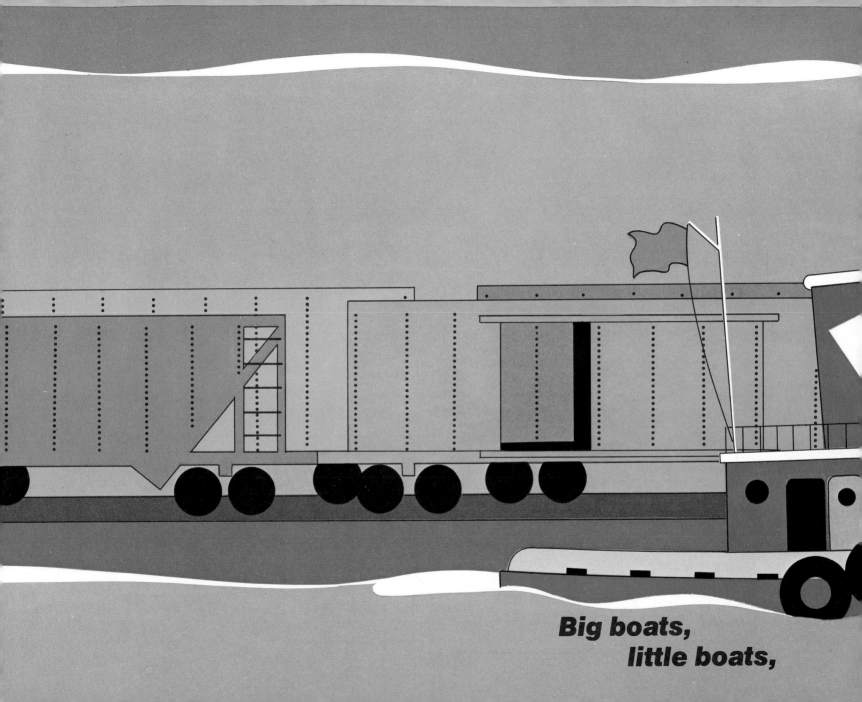

**Big boats,
little boats,**

DONNA PATRICIA

long, low-lying barges,

fast police boats, and
slow-moving lighters
crowd the water.

The tugboat is the busiest boat in the harbor.

Tugs push.
Tugs tow.

*Tugs guide big boats
to their docks*

and out again.

In the harbor the fireboat is ready for an emergency

or a celebration.

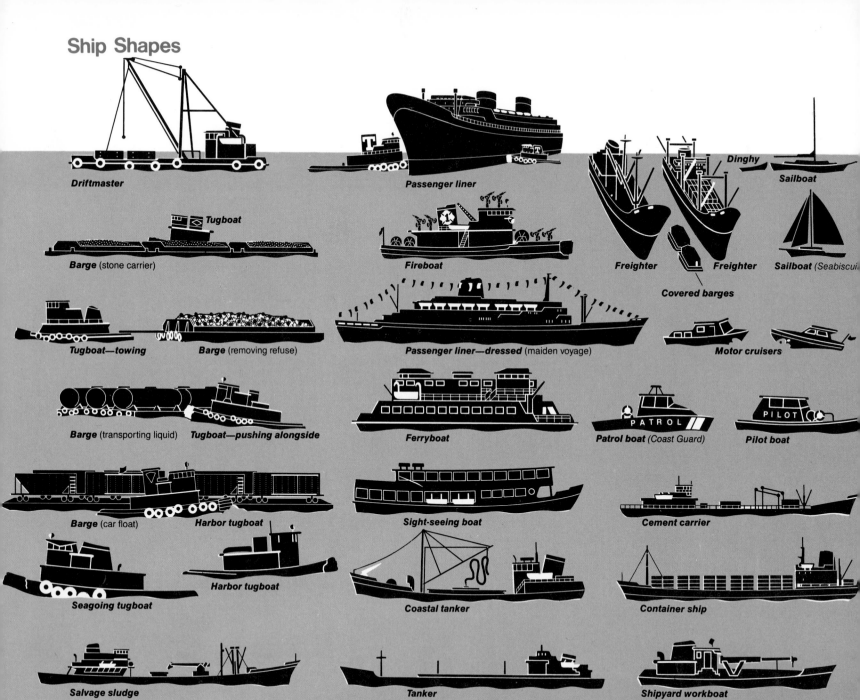

Ship Shapes

Driftmaster

Passenger liner

Dinghy

Sailboat

Tugboat

Barge (stone carrier)

Fireboat

Freighter

Freighter

Sailboat (*Seabiscu*

Covered barges

Tugboat—towing

Barge (removing refuse)

Passenger liner—dressed (maiden voyage)

Motor cruisers

Barge (transporting liquid) **Tugboat—pushing alongside**

Ferryboat

Patrol boat (*Coast Guard*)

PATROL

PILOT

Pilot boat

Barge (car float) **Harbor tugboat**

Sight-seeing boat

Cement carrier

Seagoing tugboat

Harbor tugboat

Coastal tanker

Container ship

Salvage sludge

Tanker

Shipyard workboat